The
Story YOUR
of
SOUL

Recovering the Pearl of
Your True Identity

D0090004

ELIZABETH CLARE PROPHET

SUMMIT UNIVERSITY  PRESS®

THE STORY OF YOUR SOUL
Recovering the Pearl of Your True Identity
by Elizabeth Clare Prophet
Copyright © 2007 Summit Publications, Inc.
All rights reserved

For information, contact Summit University Press, 63 Summit Way, Gardiner, MT 59030.
Tel: 1-800-245-5445 or 406-848-9500
Web site: www.summituniversitypress.com

Library of Congress Catalog Number: 2006939850
ISBN: 978-1-932890-11-2

SUMMIT UNIVERSITY ❧ PRESS

Cover design by George Foster   www.fostercovers.com

Printed in the United States of America.
12 11 10 09 08 07   6 5 4 3 2 1

The
Story
of YOUR
SOUL

Note: The flower image used throughout this book represents the six-petaled seat-of-the-soul chakra, or energy center. The seat-of-the-soul chakra is located at spiritual levels midway between the base of the spine and the navel.

The soul is anchored to the physical body through this chakra. It is the point where we make contact with our soul and receive her impressions and guidance. The energy of the soul chakra quickens our intuition and sense of freedom.

Contents

A Note from the Editors

Elizabeth Clare Prophet frequently taught about the profound opportunity that is given to every soul to fulfill an extraordinary purpose. This book is a compilation from the author's published and unpublished teachings given over many years. Affirmations, meditations, questions and exercises have been added for self-reflection and to enrich your experience in book discussion groups.

We would love to hear from you about your experiences and insights from reading the book and experimenting with the spiritual tools. Please write to us at Pocket Guides to Practical Spirituality, 63 Summit Way, Gardiner, Montana 59030 or contact us at MyStory@summituniversitypress.com.

The Editors
Summit University Press

Our birth is but a sleep and a forgetting:
The Soul that rises with us, our life's Star,
Hath had elsewhere its setting,
And cometh from afar:
Not in entire forgetfulness,
And not in utter nakedness,
But trailing clouds of glory do we come
From God, who is our home.

—WILLIAM WORDSWORTH

PART 1

Who Am I?
Why Am I Here?
Where Am I Going?

The Story of Your Soul

Imagine you are a prince. One day your parents, the king and queen, send you on a mission to a distant land. You must find a pearl guarded by a hungry dragon.

You take off your royal robe and leave the kingdom of your parents. You journey to this distant land, putting on dirty clothing and disguising yourself as one of her people.

Somehow the people of this land discover that you are a foreigner. They give you food that makes you forget your royal birth and makes you believe that you are one of them. You sink into a deep sleep.

Your parents see your plight and send you a letter that tells you to awaken. It reminds you of your quest to recover the pearl. You remember who you are, a child of kings. You quickly subdue the dragon, retrieve the pearl and depart, leaving the dirty clothing behind.

When you return to your native land, you
see your royal robe, which reminds you of the
splendor you lived in before. The garment speaks
to you, telling you that it belongs to the one
who is stronger than all human beings. You put
on your royal robe once more and return to your
father's palace.[1]

Within this story about the quest for a pearl
lies the elusive answer to the perennial
questions Who am I? Why am I here? Where am
I going? Based on a divinely inspired Gnostic poem
called "The Hymn of the Pearl," this story is an
allegory for the profound mystery of your soul's
journey from her first abode down to earth and
back again.

It is the story of the soul who descends from
the spiritual realms into the earthly planes of illu-
sion and loses the memory of her* origin. She faces
the trials and tribulations of the lower life until she
responds to the call from Home—the call that leads
to her ascent and culminates in union with her God.

---

*The soul of man and woman is feminine in relation to the
masculine, or spirit, portion of being. The soul is therefore
often referred to as "she."

I believe this to be the story of your soul journeying out from the highest point of consciousness to these planes here below and then returning with the pearl. The pearl represents your soul's knowledge of her true identity. Retrieving the pearl and bringing it Home symbolizes her integration with her true identity, her Higher Self.

 ## Life's Grand Design

Each soul is part of a larger scheme. The Creator chooses the precise moment in history for each soul to come to earth to take part in the divine outplaying of the decades and the centuries. This timetable of the conception and birth of every child is part of God's grand design of life—a design so exact that at the moment of conception the genes in each tiny embryo are already suited to the specific soul who will inhabit it.

Consider how wondrously you were made, how God cared for you personally, how your own Father-Mother God ordained your conception, your parents, your life, your purpose and your reason for being.

But God was not only thinking of you before you were born. He was already thinking of whose great-great-grandmother and great-great-grandfather you might be. The plan of the mind of God, that great cosmic computer, is so vast that none of us can even begin to comprehend it.

So if you have ever felt like an unwanted child, you can let your soul be healed of that burden. For

Try looking upon your self more as God does. For God is never confused and can only see Himself in you.

— HAFIZ

your Father-Mother loved you in the beginning, has loved you through your life's trials, and will continue to love you all the way Home.

As each of us makes this journey, we have a mission to fulfill and a unique identity to manifest. God did not create us out of a cosmic cookie cutter and stamp us out to be exactly like him. Rather, each one of us has been endowed with a distinct blueprint, which is shared only with our other half, our twin flame. This blueprint is a seed idea from God that urges us to pursue our journey, that pushes us onward and upward, that pushes us to strive.

Striving toward the Goal

When we are not striving and not working toward lesser and greater goals that lead us to our final destination, our soul is unhappy. That unhappiness may show up as sickness, boredom or self-deception. It can take the form of moodiness or little irritations and problems with family members or others—things that we don't associate with our soul's dissatisfaction.

Yet our soul is impressing upon our outer awareness, "You are stifling me. You are not fulfilling the purpose for which I was born. And I will not leave you in comfort. I will make you without comfort until you return to follow the inner plan of life."

Our divine plan is waiting for our free-will confirmation. If we believe in predestination, we may think we don't have to do anything—it's all going to happen anyway. But in reality, because of the gift of free will, we can choose to implement our divine plan or not.

I can remember when all I knew about my divine plan was that I had to do something for God in this life, that I had a mission and I had to find out what it was. And since I didn't know what it was, my mission became finding it out. So each day during my childhood and my schooling, I would try to study and pursue those subjects which, if mastered, would lead me closer to the knowledge of my life's mission.

Do you know your mission, your divine plan? One clue is that your mission is often your passion. So you can ask yourself what you are passionate about. Another clue is that your mission usually involves perfecting the talents that God has placed within your soul.

Above and beyond all else, the purpose of life, the answer to "Why am I here?" is to find God—in yourself, in your talents, in your calling and in your service to life. It is to endow everything you do with God's Spirit. Endowing everything with God's Spirit is making his Spirit permanent in you. This is the journey of integration back to the kingdom of your Father-Mother God.

Your Soul's Divine Potential

The following glimpse of the "pearl" can serve as a road map for your personal journey. It can also help to answer the questions "Who am I?" and "Where am I going?"

The soul is the living potential of God—the part of you that is mortal but can become immortal. She gains immortality through her journey.

Remembering that the pearl represents the soul's knowledge of her Higher Self, you can meditate on the following picture, the Chart of Your Divine Self. It illustrates your spiritual anatomy—your divine nature and direct relationship with God.

This Chart shows three distinct levels of consciousness. In relationship to the story of your soul's journey, you might look at the lower figure as your soul's consciousness and the middle figure as the consciousness of your Higher Self, the guide for your journey. The upper figure can be seen as the birthright of royal consciousness that is yours when you finally return to your heavenly abode.

THE CHART OF YOUR DIVINE SELF

The I AM Presence

The highest level of consciousness is represented by the upper figure—the Presence of God with you, the Father-Mother God—the all-loving, all-knowing, all-pure, all-powerful God. This is the I AM Presence, the Presence of God individualized in each of us. It is your *personalized* I AM THAT I AM, the name that God revealed to Moses at Mount Sinai when God said, "This is my name forever and this is my memorial unto all generations."[2]

God saw us in the plight of having forgotten where we came from and who we were in the beginning. So he gave us a memory of himself, a memorial. He gave each one of us an I AM Presence—a portion of his being and consciousness. (See the image on page 10.) This is the consciousness you will put on when you arrive at the palace of your father, just like the prince in the story.

Surrounding your I AM Presence are seven concentric spheres of pulsating spiritual energy. These spheres, called the causal body, contain the record of all the good works you have ever performed, stored as your treasures in heaven, your cosmic bank account. No two causal bodies are exactly alike, because their shimmering spheres reflect the unique spiritual attainment of the individual soul.

Your Higher Self

The middle figure in the Chart represents your Higher Self. This is your inner teacher, your dearest friend and the voice of conscience that guides, warns and comforts you on the homeward journey. The Higher Self will give you unerring direction if you will tune in to this still small voice within you.

Jesus discovered the Higher Self to be "the Christ" and Gautama discovered it to be "the Buddha." Thus, the Higher Self is sometimes called the Inner Christ (or Christ Self) or the Inner Buddha. Christian mystics sometimes refer to it as the inner man of the heart or the Inner Light. And the Upanishads mysteriously describe it as a being the "size of a thumb" who "dwells deep within the heart." Whether we call it the Christ, the Buddha, the Atman or the Tao, each of us is meant to become one with our Higher Self.

The Crystal Cord and Threefold Flame

Looking at the Chart, you will see a ribbon of white light descending from your I AM Presence to your heart. Called the crystal cord or silver cord, this is the crystal clear river of life mentioned in the Book of Revelation.[3]

It's like a mighty river of energy—energy that empowers us to think, feel, reason, experience life and grow spiritually. But when we turn our attention away from those things that contribute to our soul's purpose, that energy starts to fragment. Rivulets of energy flow away from the mainstream and the blueprint of our life, and this can sap us of the full strength we need to carry out our mission.

Your crystal cord nourishes and sustains the flame of God anchored at spiritual levels in the secret, or hidden, chamber of the heart. This flame is called the threefold flame or divine spark—literally a spark of sacred fire from God's own heart kindled within you. By fully accessing the power, the wisdom and the love of your threefold flame, you can fulfill your soul's reason for being.

Imagine the secret chamber of your heart as your private meditation room. It's the place where you can commune with your Inner Buddha, your Inner Christ. Jesus was referring to the secret chamber of the heart when he spoke of going into the closet to pray. The mystic Teresa of Avila called this closet her "interior castle." Truly entering this closet is going into another dimension of consciousness.

Your Four Lower Bodies

The lower figure in the Chart represents your soul in embodiment evolving in time and space. Your soul is clothed in garments of four lower bodies, though only the physical body is shown. These are four energy fields, or sheaths of consciousness. They are like colanders stacked inside each other, each vibrating in a different dimension. They surround your soul and function as her vehicles of expression in the material world.

Aside from your physical body, you have an emotional, or desire, body—the body of your feelings and desires. You also have a mental body, the body of thinking and reasoning. The etheric body, the highest vibrating of the four, is your memory body.

When your four lower bodies are in alignment, like a set of colanders with their holes lined up, the light of your I AM Presence can flow freely through you. So part of the work of the spiritual path is gaining balance in these bodies—physical, psychological, mental and spiritual balance.

The Ascension

The goal of each soul's journey in time and space is to permanently unite with her Higher Self and I AM Presence in the ritual of the ascension. This is the integration of the three levels of consciousness shown in the Chart. In Western religion, we say we've entered heaven. In Eastern terms, we've attained liberation or *parinirvana*. According to Gnosticism, we have reclaimed our pearl and returned to our divine parents. These are just different ways of describing the soul's state of consciousness once she has ascended back to the heart of God.

A powerful way to accelerate your journey is to invoke spiritual light, including the violet flame. The spiritual energy of the violet flame is shown surrounding the lower figure in the Chart. The violet flame is the color and frequency of spiritual

The Trikaya, or Three Bodies of the Buddha

Some Buddhists believe that each aspirant to Buddhahood successively "puts on" three bodies. He begins at the level of the Nirmanakaya, called the Body of Transformation. This is the physical form of an embodied Buddha, such as Gautama Buddha. It is also the refined, purified body of the striving disciple evolving on the spiritual path. In the Chart, it relates to the lower figure.

The aspirant then puts on the Sambhogakaya—the Body of Bliss or the Body of Inspiration. This relates to the Buddha Self, or Christ Self, corresponding to the middle figure in the Chart.

Next, he puts on the Dharmakaya, which is called the Body of the Law or Body of First Cause—the timeless, permanent body of the Buddha. It corresponds to the upper figure in the Chart.

When the three bodies of the Buddha are united and experienced simultaneously, they are known as the Vajrakaya. In Sanskrit *vajra* means "the diamond," which is the symbol of the ascended state.

The union of these three bodies correlates with the full integration of the soul with her divine image—the Christ Self and I AM Presence—and her final ascent to her God.

light that stimulates the qualities of mercy, justice, freedom and transmutation. It can be invoked to purify your four lower bodies and consume negative thoughts and feelings. The Chart also depicts a protective tube of white light that descends directly from your I AM Presence in answer to your prayers. (See pages 102–115 for how to give calls for the violet flame and the tube of light.)

The Chart, therefore, can be seen as a pictorial version of the story of the prince—or the story of your soul, reclaiming the pearl and finally returning to the kingdom of her Father-Mother God.

Soul Reflections

1. Imagine yourself as the prince in the story. Where do you see yourself in the journey? Awakening from a deep sleep? Fighting dragons? Reclaiming the pearl?

2. What do you consider to be your unique mission?

   If you know what it is, might there be an aspect beyond what you've been doing?

   If you don't know, think about what you enjoy doing, the things that give you the greatest sense

of fulfillment, and your gifts and talents. Or ask
five people who know you well what they think
your special gift is. Reflect on all these things to
see if they give you any insights about your
mission.

3. How is your soul speaking to you right now
    through your body, mind and emotions?

    How might she be trying to get your attention?

    Write down your thoughts. Then as you continue
    reading this book, be alert to how you might work
    with your soul to resolve these things and make
    your life better and more fulfilling.

4. In what ways does the Chart of Your Divine Self
    expand your understanding of yourself as a
    spiritual being?

PART 2

The Continuum
of the Soul

 Free Will

To understand the spiritual path, it's essential to begin at the beginning—to realize that originally we were all light and dwelled in a Spirit cosmos. We asked for the gift of free will, God granted our request and we came to the reaches of a material universe. We gradually became enmeshed in denser and denser spheres until we found ourselves embodied on this small planet, somewhere out in left field, far away from our spiritual home.

Free will is God's gift to man for self-determination. It allows us to create, to be co-creators with God and with one another. We can use the divine light and energy flowing to us in whatever way we choose. We can fulfill our desires for good or ill. We can change things. Every single day and moment, in everything we do, we are exercising our free will. So free will is the pivot of existence and true being.

God understands that we will come in contact with all things in this world. We will learn our lessons, pass some of our tests and not necessarily all, overcome some temptations and not necessarily others. The fruit of all these experiences is our self-mastery and a greater love that intensifies within us as we are gradually liberated from the lower self and unite with our Higher Self.

People sometimes think in terms of predestination and destiny. But in reality, we determine the outcome of our fate every day by our free-will choices of what we do with our circumstances. And *circumstances* is another word for karma.

 Karma

Karma is a Sanskrit word meaning "act," "action," "work" or "deed." Hinduism and Buddhism teach that the law of karma is a universal law of cause and effect that affects everyone. As Newton's third law of motion states, "For every action there is an equal and opposite reaction." To put it in simple terms: What goes around, comes around. Whatever you do comes full circle to your doorstep for resolution.

The law of karma is inseparable from life on earth. Almost everything we do is setting something in motion that is going to have ramifications. An idle word, a careless remark can affect someone for a day or a week. We have set up a cause; it is in motion. Likewise, we can bring joy and comfort, learning, or a nugget of truth that gives someone a burst of awareness. These are also causes we've set in motion by our free will—causes that will ripple on and affect others. So we begin to see that we are absolutely responsible for what we think, feel, say and do—or don't do.

Another definition of karma is unconditional love. It is precisely because God loves us that he allows our

Karma is of great importance, but of greater gravity is the choice. Karma is but the condition of the choice.

— LEAVES OF MORYA'S GARDEN

karma to return to us. Being on the receiving end of causes we have set in motion shows us the consequences of our actions and inactions. We learn to do unto others as we would have them do unto us, and this helps our soul develop. Thus the law of karma is the law of love. It teaches us compassion, as well as humility, empathy, mercy and sensitivity to life. It brings remorse and reconciliation. It teaches us to love as no other process can or does.

 ## Dealing with Karma Day by Day

Every morning the bundle of karma we have been assigned for the day greets us at our doorstep. We are allotted a portion of good karma based on the love, comfort and enlightenment we have extended to life in the past. Likewise, a certain portion of our negative karma also arrives for resolution.

Good karma can manifest as anything from a supportive circle of family and friends to genius, aptitudes and talents. Our positive karma and momentums can even launch us like a rocket ship on the pathway of our soul's mission.

Negative karma can manifest as anything from destructive habit patterns to disease, accidents or difficult relationships. When negative karma descends, we have a choice. We can either follow the tendency of our karma and our past, or we can challenge it. We can say, "I am not the victim of my stars, my fate or my karma. I am a new being. And this day I determine that I will be all-love in action. If I hated my neighbor yesterday, I will love my neighbor today. This is my free will, and I choose to change my course for a victory in this life."

> *Rise early and think upon your deeds, and of the world to come; for you may be certain that the fruits of all your deeds will think upon you.*
>
> – ANCIENT SANSKRIT VERSE

According to Western thinking, pleasure is good and pain is bad. Experiencing the return of negative karma is sometimes painful, but pain can be a teacher, a purifier. Pain is necessary at our level of development—it teaches us to eliminate the causes of pain and to set in motion causes of bliss on the path to our reunion with God.

Balancing karma is a joyous path because you are paying your karmic debts fully and finally. It's similar to how you feel when you can pay all your bills at the end of the month.

"Pay as you go" is a guiding principle of the soul on the spiritual path. Even though you don't think about it as karma, your soul knows and she expresses profound joy to be paying her debts with dignity. You are being responsible and accountable; you are alleviating pain and serving to set life free. This puts you on the right side of the law of karma.

When you get on the right side of karma, it will work for you. It will open the door for your blessings to continually multiply and increase, because you are affecting many others in a positive way.

Ideally, we're balancing karma every day and not making any new negative karma. And we can balance previous karma by good works, devotion, prayer and the violet flame.

The violet flame is a unique spiritual energy that transmutes, or transforms, negative karma. To understand how the violet flame works, we can consider the ancient Oriental art of Feng Shui. According to Feng Shui, clutter and the arrangement of your physical surroundings determine the flow of energy in your environment. That flow powerfully affects your health, your abundance, your relationships and the very course of your life. In the same way, karmic clutter in your body, mind and emotions can cause the energy within and around you to stagnate.

We all have some karmic clutter since we have all created negative energy. This energy has collected and then calcified in our physical, mental and emotional worlds. As a result of this karma, we don't feel as light, free, happy, vibrant and spiritual as we could. When we pray for the violet flame to surround us, it can consume the debris within and between the atoms of our being. (See pages 106–115 for more on the violet flame and balancing karma.)

So each day we can look at the karma that has returned to us and decide how we will respond to it. Remember, it's not what happens to us in life, it's how we react to it that makes all the difference.

 ## Lifetimes of Opportunity

The law of karma implies reincarnation. Karma necessitates rebirth because we are not able to reap all the effects of our karma in a single lifetime. Instead, we must come back multiple times to experience the return of, or compensation for, all that we have done. These lifetimes stretch across the ages because we must reembody at the same time as others with whom we have karma.

Everything you are today you have been building for centuries. Your talents, achievements, good deeds and love are all cumulative, just as your negative manifestations are cumulative. And we need this cumulative experience. That's why God set up the system of reincarnation. A single lifetime, whether lived to age 9 or 90 or 900, is just not enough time for the soul to mature to the levels required for her to recover her pearl and go Home.

Many cultures and traditions have treated reincarnation as a given. For example, the earliest known Kabbalistic text, *Sefer ha-Bahir,* published around 1180, uses a dialogue about reincarnation to explain that terrible things happen to good people because of what they have done in previous lives. So if we think that some people get away with everything while we get away with nothing, we just have to realize that the law of karma operates automatically and without prejudice in the life of every soul.

We are reaping today what we might have sown five minutes ago, yesterday or ten thousand years ago. We don't know how long it will take for our actions to come full circle and demand that we make them right. But God knows, and his law is unerring, unfailing and always just.

You are a soul and a fiery spirit, a spiritual being, wearing garments of flesh like an overcoat you have put on in this life and many times before. Your soul predated this body and will exist afterwards.

> *I believe I shall, in some shape or other, always exist, and, with all the inconveniences human life is liable to, I shall not object to a new edition of mine, hoping, however, that the errata of the last may be corrected.*
>
> – BENJAMIN FRANKLIN

You just use the physical form until it is no longer functioning. That's how natural reincarnation is!

Thus, the creation of a new body is not the creation of a new soul. God isn't waiting around for the moment of conception to quick! hurry up!

get out the dough, form another soul and pop it into the womb so that it will be there when that child is born.

Rather, the soul that we are today is the same soul that separated from God, got disconnected in a big way and has been trying to find her way back. Each time our soul prepares to reembody, she is filled with the sense of going back to pick up dropped stitches, finish her work and then give the world something of herself—an artistic creation, a gift of love and sweetness, kindness or some great achievement.

We sense ourselves as extensions of God. We sense that we must be about the business of our Father-Mother and we must fulfill our divine plan. This is the inner sense of karma and, beyond karma, the fiery destiny of our soul.

 ## Memories of Other Lifetimes

Some people have remembered a past life, while others have not. But those who think they haven't remembered a past life sometimes have a strong sense of familiarity with a certain situation or location or with a specific person or group of people. At times they may have an instantaneous dislike or even a sense of danger around someone. Or they may feel that they have known an individual for a long time, finding it easy to get to know that person, even if they have just met.

We have little hints of other lives, but God in his mercy draws a curtain of forgetfulness over us when we enter the birth canal. This is a mercy, because we have an assignment for this life and shouldn't spend our days wishing we were who we used to be or longing for the good old days. We need to be locked in to the here and now and recognize what an opportunity it is to be in embodiment to work out the karma of the past.

One spring day when I was four years old, I was playing in my sandbox in the picket-fenced play yard my father had built for me. It was my own little world inside the larger world of our backyard in Red Bank, New Jersey. I was alone, letting the sand slip through my fingers and watching the fluffy clouds roll by.

Then gradually, gently, the scene began to change. As though someone had turned the dial on a radio, I was on another frequency—playing in the sand along the Nile River in Egypt. It was just as real as my play yard in Red Bank and just as familiar. I was idling away the hours, splashing in the water and feeling the warm sand on my body. My Egyptian mother was nearby. Somehow this, too, was my world. I had known that river forever.

How did I know it was Egypt and the Nile? Knowing it was part of the experience. Perhaps my conscious mind made the connection because my present-day parents had put a map of the world above my toy chest and I already knew the names of most of the countries.

After some time (I don't know how long), it was as though the dial turned again and I was back at home in my little play yard. I wasn't dizzy, I wasn't dazed. I was back in the present, very much aware that I had been somewhere else. So I jumped up and ran to look for my mother, and I found her standing at the kitchen stove. I blurted out my story, then asked her, "What happened?" She sat me down, looked at me and said, "You have remembered a past life." With those words, she opened another dimension.

Instead of ridiculing me or denying what I had experienced, she spoke to me in terms a child could understand: "Our body is like a coat we wear. It gets worn out before we finish what we have to do. So God gives us a new mommy and a new daddy, and we are born again so we can finish the work God sent us to do and finally return to our home of light in heaven."

I understood that even though we get a new body, we still have the same soul. And our soul remembers the past, even though our conscious mind may not.

We usually don't remember our past lives because it would be a psychological burden. God lets us start anew with a clean white page each time we take embodiment. And when, in the full maturity of our souls, we are ready to understand our responsibilities in life, we begin to realize that we are a continuum.

When we finally get tired and fed up with coming back for yet another round and we want a higher way of life, we will accelerate on the homeward path. We'll come to terms with this life and all the things that are in it. And we'll make it our goal to get off the merry-go-round of rebirth for the last time.

The Soul's Graduation from Earth

As previously mentioned, when the soul fulfills the purpose of her journey on earth, she returns to God in the ritual of the ascension. The ascension is the culmination of embodiments of the soul's service to life.

In order for the soul to attain this final union with God, she must have fulfilled certain requirements. Primarily, she needs to balance at least 51 percent of her karma; complete her mission; balance the love, wisdom and power of her threefold flame; and become one with her Christ Self.

> *The path of the ascension is the path of Love.*
>
> – SERAPIS BEY

When your soul ascends back to God, you will be free from the rounds of karma and rebirth. You will be an "ascended" master. You'll join the many adepts and saints of East and West who have risen out of every culture, every religion and united with their Christ Self and I AM Presence. Some are known—like Jesus, Gautama Buddha,

Kuan Yin, Krishna, Padre Pio, Saint Thérèse of Lisieux, Kuthumi. Most are unknown. But all have accelerated in consciousness to become one with God.

Therefore the ascension is the goal of life on earth; it is our reason for being. We come into incarnation over and over again until we finally realize what the goal is and follow the steps of initiation to return to the heart of God.

We don't ascend all at once, but we ascend in increments, day by day, as we pass the tests of life and win our individual victories. Our thoughts, our feelings, our daily deeds are all weighed in the balance.

If you comb through the scriptures of the world, you will find examples of the ascension. It may be called soul liberation, parinirvana, *mahasamadhi* —all states of consciousness that represent the acceleration of the very atoms and electrons of one's being. So when we read of "going up," as Jesus and Elijah are described, it means increasing in vibration. It is not a literal up or down but a lesser or greater momentum of cosmic consciousness that manifests within a person.

God transcends himself moment by moment,

hour by hour. This self-transcending God is reflected in the expanding cosmos, and it is also reflected in man. For no matter what level of attainment an individual reaches, he or she will usually set a further goal. So the ascension is not the end of life or the end of striving toward goals. Cosmic consciousness is ever appearing.

Soul Reflections

1. In what areas of your life do you feel you are exercising free will?

    In what areas do you feel locked in by karma?

    Does your perception of the world around you change when you consider that your free-will choices determine your fate? In what ways?

2. What situations or relationships in your life do you think might be the result of good karma and why?

    How can you best handle any negative karma that's returning to you?

3. What gifts or talents do you have that might be carried over from a previous life?

   Have you felt compelled to do certain things that might be dropped stitches from another life? How did those things enhance your life experience?

4. What are your thoughts or feelings about the concept that every soul is destined to ascend?

PART 3

Navigating the Change Called Death

The Change Called Death

The first thing you need to know about death is that death is not real. Yes, it is the process whereby the systems of the physical body shut down—the heart, the brain and the rest. But it is not the end of you. It is not the end of your existence, your consciousness or the continuity of your soul.

When your soul concludes a lifetime on earth, the I AM Presence withdraws the crystal cord and your three-fold flame returns to the etheric plane, to the heart of your Holy Christ Self. Your soul, clothed in her etheric body, gravitates to the highest level of consciousness that she has attained during her incarnations.

Although it is not the end

Life is real!
Life is earnest!
And the grave is
not its goal;
Dust thou art,
to dust returnest,
was not spoken
of the soul.

— HENRY WADSWORTH
LONGFELLOW

of existence, death *is* a major change. If you think of the biggest change that has happened to you in this lifetime and multiply it by a hundred, you will begin to understand the immensity of this transition. And the major adjustment is that you no longer have a physical body.

Without a physical body, your opportunity to act in the earth plane comes to an end. You no longer have the ability to make amends with people. No opportunity to resolve problems or misunderstandings with your family and others. No opportunity to say, "I'm sorry" or "I love you."

So it is not the cessation of life in the physical body that needs to concern us. Instead, we should be concerned whether we will have accomplished everything we wanted to do—for our children, our family, our loved ones, for our community, humanity and God.

 Near-Death Experiences

Near-death experiences (NDEs) show that we are more than our physical bodies. While many people easily understand this, it is surprising how many others identify almost totally with their physical body. When someone has a near-death experience, it usually reassures him that there is life after death. Widespread publicity of near-death experiences has also given comfort and consolation to millions of people who have not had an NDE themselves.

Many years ago, a young woman I know had a near-death experience when she was in a car accident. When she woke up in the hospital, she could not remember the event. All she could recall was flying through a vacuum, a dark void, with brilliant lights moving toward her.

"I came out into this peaceful place," she said. "I remember standing before this beautiful being that I thought of as God. The form it took was that of a loving older man. It felt like the very essence of this image was light. It was such a brilliant, bright light! And he kept saying the words over and over, 'Are you prepared to die?'

"When I woke up in that hospital, I just kept hearing those words, 'Are you prepared to die?' He wasn't actually speaking them—everything was a vibration.

"He was showing me that I was a part of him and I was a part of that light. I was a part of God, and God had given me light to use in whatever way I pleased. He showed me what I had been doing with the light. And he asked me if I had accomplished what I wanted to accomplish in this life.

"I felt so much gratitude for being shown that what I was doing was not worthwhile. I had the feeling of begging to go back to really do something with my life."

Of course, not everyone who "dies" and is resuscitated has a near-death experience. But for those who do, there is surely a reason. A person could be chosen for the experience because someone up there, perhaps an angel or an ascended master, loves him and wants to tell him that he's on the wrong track; and if he keeps going on that track, he's going to wind up in a bad place. Some have earned the experience, and perhaps they need it for their soul's evolution—to remind them that they came to earth for a reason.

You, too, have a reason for being. And whatever else may be your specific calling or profession in life, the ultimate reason for being is to love, to set life free, to balance your karma and to attain reunion with God. How, when, why, where and with whom you're going to do this remains for you to discover by your gift of free will.

We Make Our Own Heaven or Hell

When the soul makes her transition in the change called death, she goes to the inner level for which she has fitted herself. She may be assigned to levels of light because she has contributed to the momentums of light on earth. Or she may be assigned to lower levels because she has contributed to lower momentums.

Some religious traditions say that as we are when we die, so we are after we die. Revelation 22:11 says, "He that is unjust, let him be unjust still: and he which is filthy, let him be filthy still: and he that is righteous, let him be righteous still: and he that is holy, let him be holy still."

The Zohar, the main text of the Jewish mystical tradition, says the soul's journey beyond her earthly life is determined by the type of *devekut* she pursues during her life on earth. *Devekut* is mystical cleaving to God. The soul chooses her own fate by cleaving to either holy forces or unholy forces. "It is the path taken by man in this world that determines the path of the soul on her departure."[4] So the more you have loved and pursued God and his will in your life, the more light you have garnered and the more congruent you are with the octaves of light.

When a person passes on and has not earned his ascension, he must prepare to return to embodiment again. Some souls are taken to the etheric retreats between embodiments to learn how to further develop their existing talents and to acquire new ones for future service.

The etheric octave is the realm of perfection that many call heaven. There are thirty-three levels of the etheric octave, each exceeding the previous one in intensity of light and manifestation of

> *I sent my Soul*
> *through the*
> *Invisible,*
> *Some letter of that*
> *After-life to spell:*
> *And by and by*
> *my Soul return'd*
> *to me,*
> *And answer'd*
> *'I Myself am*
> *Heav'n and Hell.'*
>
> — THE RUBAIYAT OF
> OMAR KHAYYAM

perfection. The first level is like a kindergarten where good souls go who haven't made much negative karma but are not adept in their pursuit of the spiritual path. Often these souls are good religious people who have not strayed outside the narrow bands of their own orthodox traditions.

But all who pass on do not reach the etheric retreats and schoolrooms of the heaven-world. Many go to the astral plane.

The astral plane, which is often called purgatory, or death and hell, also has thirty-three levels. They descend in order of intensification of darkness and the types of people there. The first few levels of the astral plane resemble certain areas on earth—places that are inharmonious, dark, tied to materialism or sensuality or to various addictions. The bottom of the astral plane, at the thirty-third level, is the realm called hell—an extremely dark place where the most vicious abide.

But even if we go to the astral plane after death, it doesn't mean that we have reached the end of opportunity. Angels, messengers of God, will come to us and ask us to go with them to higher planes.

I have prayed for many souls after they have

died, and I am often allowed to see what happens to them. Some people reject or ignore the angels; they are much happier continuing with whatever they are doing. Others awaken, see the truth and realize that they must go with the angels to higher realms where they can prepare for rebirth. The souls that choose to remain in the astral plane usually reincarnate directly from that level. They come back basically as they were—with the same habits, the same desires, the same momentums.

Therefore it is important to pray for those who pass on so that they can be cut free by angels and taken to the highest place they can go. When the soul is out of embodiment, her hope for progress is in the etheric retreats.

Since some souls don't have enough attainment to make it to the octaves of light on their own, they wait until someone in embodiment makes the calls to the angels to rescue them. In Catholicism, this is the real intent of giving prayers for the dead—to pray for the departed so that they may be taken to higher realms. Similarly, *The Tibetan Book of the Dead* contains prayers that are read to the dead for consecutive days to guide the one who has left his body and preach to him not to fall into dark vibrations.

 Past-Life Review

Soon after the change called death, our soul is brought before the Karmic Board, a court of eight cosmic beings of light who assist us in reviewing our past life. Our Holy Christ Self stands with us as our advocate and helps us to understand how we have assisted life, how we have harmed life, what obligations we have incurred, whether we have fulfilled our mission and where we go from here.

In the presence of the Holy Christ Self, there is no condemnation, no punishment. For when we enter the Christ mind, we ourselves pronounce the assessment of our lives and what we must do in order to rectify the wrongs.

There is a moment of all-knowingness in the presence of these wondrous beings of light when we can see clearly what we have done, if we have unfinished business, and whether or not we shall reembody. The Karmic Board tells us if we will be assigned to an etheric temple of light and where. If we are to reembody, they give us instructors who will help us prepare for the next incarnation. Then, after a stay in an etheric retreat or city of light, they will send our soul back into embodiment. Our soul will usually have a great desire to return since she knows that her mission is unfinished.

 ## Pre-Life Review

Just as we are reviewed at the end of each embodiment, we also go before the Karmic Board when we are about to be born. They review many of our past lives with us and show us why we are embodying, with which parents, for what reason, what we must fulfill, and the people with whom we must resolve our differences if we are to make progress on the spiritual path. We are told about the difficulties we will have, the positive opportunities, and the negatives we will have to challenge.

This pre-life review is a preparation for what we will need to accomplish. It is indelibly impressed upon our soul and our memory body. So when we meet people and sense that we have a responsibility to them, we are more likely to walk the last mile, even when our friends say things like, "Why do you put up with that person?" or "Why do you get involved in situations like this where everybody is using you?"

Our soul knows where her debts are, and she goes there and does what she has to do in order to be liberated from those particular ties. This doesn't mean that the tie needs to be broken after we have fulfilled our responsibility with a person. For there is a new kind of bonding, a bonding of freedom, instead of slavery to the karmic circumstance.

> *Because the soul is progressive, it never quite repeats itself, but in every act attempts the production of a new and fairer whole.*
>
> — RALPH WALDO EMERSON

From the moment of conception, an incoming soul is an active participant in forming the body she will inhabit. Throughout the entire nine months of gestation, the soul may go back and forth from her body in the womb to higher planes of existence in the heaven-world. Each time she enters her body, she anchors more of her soul substance there. As gestation progresses, the spirit, or essence, of the soul becomes a part of the blood and the cells, a part of the brain, the heart and all of the organs.

At the moment of birth (the timing of which is integral to the soul's mission), the soul comes down the spiritual birth canal, which is like a large funnel, and the threefold flame is anchored in the secret chamber of the heart. The soul is fully integrated with the body at that time, and the veil of forgetfulness is drawn over the memory body.

Soul Reflections

1. What are your thoughts about not being in a physical body? What things would you like to be sure you have done while you still have the opportunity?

2. Have you or anyone you know had a near-death experience? If so, what insights did you gain?

3. How did the concept that we make our own heaven or hell impress you? What are you contributing to your "heaven"?

4. In spite of the veil of forgetfulness, have you ever had a sense of your soul following a plan? What soul intuitions make you think that? Or what circumstances in your life might point to it?

PART 4

Keys for Your Soul's Journey

Your Soul and the Spiritual Path

Have you ever thought about the fact that in this life and past lives you might have neglected the development of your soul, choosing instead to develop your human ego? Or that you may not have nurtured your soul?

What is your soul?

Your soul is the life-essence that mirrors your human personality and the divine personality, the personality of God. Your current soul identity—your individual soul identity—reflects how you have integrated these personalities.

God intends for each soul to return to Spirit and live forever in the divine consciousness as an individualization of the God flame. God is one, but he chooses to make from his oneness single drops of light, individual sons and daughters—all part of his oneness yet distinct and unique.

We are each supremely individual in our

outlook, our likes and dislikes, and especially our attainments and what we do with our life. And our journey on the path is also individual—we each walk the path alone.

As we do this, we need to be mindful of our unique soul sensitivity and knowledge. Our souls are wise. They know the past and its application to the present and the future. They are highly sensitive and at the same time innocent and defenseless.

Our soul is vulnerable, impressionable, often colored by her surroundings, easily led astray. She suffers when subjected to violence of any kind. She is wounded by mental and emotional toxins and by physical or verbal abuse.

> *I can find nothing with which to compare the great beauty of a soul and its great capacity.*
>
> – TERESA OF AVILA

Our souls urgently need our comfort and consolation, our soothing words. They need to know that we will protect them from all harm.

We can consider our soul as the child who lives inside of us, our "inner child." And we are her parents and teachers, even as we are her students. It is our responsibility to daily impress upon the soul (1) what is right (what is real and of enduring worth and therefore must be retained) and (2) what is wrong (what is not real and not of enduring worth and therefore must be discarded).

As parents, we can lovingly care for our souls as we would care for our children. Or we can neglect our souls and become creatures of our own self-neglect—soul-neglect. The book of Proverbs says, "Train up a child in the way he should go: and when he is old, he will not depart from it." These words refer to one's soul as well as to one's offspring. We need to love and protect, instruct and discipline her on the spiritual path.

Living a Spiritual Life

So what does it mean to be on the spiritual path, to live a spiritual life? And what is spirituality? The word *spirit* comes from the Latin *spiritus,* meaning "breath," "breath of a god" or "inspiration." Spirituality is to the soul what the breath of life is to a newborn child. It infuses you with new life and vigor. It empowers you to love and nourish yourself and others.

Spirituality is being able to sustain a working relationship with God. It doesn't matter what you call that God—the Higher Self, the Inner Light, the Buddha, the Tao, Brahman, Adonai. It's possible for each of us to get in touch, and stay in touch, with the universal power of God.

People have often asked me how they can do this: How can I find inner peace in the midst of outer turmoil? How can I handle the stresses that come up during the day and still keep my spiritual attunement? For example, how can I be spiritual when I have to work overtime and my child is sick and waiting for me? Or when I just found out that I lost my job? Well, it's true that it isn't easy. And there's no one I know who doesn't have trials; we all do. But there are spiritual solutions to today's challenges.

Spirituality is a process of self-mastery. It's like climbing a mountain. There are many ways to reach the summit of being. And each trail up the mountain will give you a different perspective—a new way of understanding who God is and who you are.

We are climbing that mountain each day, all day, not just when we take time out to meditate, watch a beautiful sunset, or give prayers and devotions. Every day we can remember to teach our soul—the little child who is destined to become the Christ Child. We can lead our soul, even as we are led by our Holy Christ Self, and restore her to heavenly patterns. The following keys can help us in this process.

Keys for Your Soul's Journey

1. Forgive Yourself

2. Forgive Others

3. Make Friends in Heaven

4. Learn While Your Body Sleeps

5. Be Aware of the Not-Self

6. Work on Your Psychology

7. Talk with God

 1. Forgive Yourself

The way to achieve harmony with all parts of the psyche is through mercy and forgiveness—mercy whereby you forgive yourself, mercy whereby you forgive others.

All of us are human, and we've all done things we're not proud of. So forgive yourself for being human and for making mistakes. Forgive yourself for the errors and karma of your previous lifetimes, whether you remember them or not.

We all have had to go through our experiences in the best way we knew how at the time. Sometimes it wasn't the most perfect way, but that is the process of learning—experiencing, going through trial and error, and then finally coming out on top.

Never condemn yourself for your shortcomings and mistakes. Just resolve to do better the next time. If you condemn yourself even a little, it's like poking a hole in a water bottle. The water slowly but surely leaks out. No matter how much water you put in the bottle, it will not stay full. That's what happens to your aura, your energy, when you allow anything or anyone, including yourself, to condemn you so that you feel you are not worthy of God's love.

Your soul *is* worthy—she is worthy of God's love and his forgiveness. So you can ask God for forgiveness for all wrongs you have ever committed. When you receive forgiveness, something is lifted, some percentage of the weight of karma, the burden of the act itself. Therefore forgiveness is an important part of balancing karma.

You have to forgive yourself to receive God's

> *Self-forgiveness is a great birth.... It is the state of being that arises from our willingness to accept, without judgment, all of who we are, our seeming shortcomings as well as our innate glory.*
>
> — ROBIN CASARJIAN

forgiveness. If you truly forgive yourself, you establish a magnet of forgiveness in your heart, which draws down God's forgiveness.

Accepting God's forgiveness is the foundation for resolution. If we are not resolved with God, then we are not resolved with the God within us or in our fellowman.

So make your peace with God and with every part of life you have ever wronged and every part of life that has ever wronged you. Forgive yourself and move on with the day-by-day process of putting on your Christhood.

Soul Reflections

Finding forgiveness

Take a moment to recall something that you have not fully forgiven yourself for. We often resist remembering painful experiences.

So if nothing comes to mind, ask your Higher Self to show you an incident. It might be breaking a promise, saying words you regret or being responsible for an accident—anything, great or small.

Ask God and anyone you may have harmed for forgiveness. Resolve to do better, and know that you are on the way to becoming your Higher Self.

Try using the following meditation and affirmation.

Imagine yourself standing under a gentle, violet-colored waterfall that washes away any sense of guilt or blame, shame or condemnation. Let the soothing water of forgiveness flow in, through and around you, giving your soul a sense of peace.

Next, repeat the following affirmation to draw down the violet-flame action of mercy and forgiveness. When you say "I AM," you are affirming God within you. See your heart becoming a magnet for forgiveness.

I AM a being of violet fire!

I AM the purity God desires!

2. Forgive Others

Forgive your friends, your enemies and all who have ever wronged you. When you send love and forgiveness to others, you are bringing resolution. You're also doing something for yourself—you're freeing yourself from entanglements of this and previous lives.

Look at the people you are tied to today. Look at your situation with your job, your family and everything that affects you. Most of us have difficult people in our lives. Sometimes we can't seem to resolve things with them and to disentangle ourselves. Often it's because we've never forgiven old hurts and old wrongs, some from previous embodiments, so they hang on. And nonforgiveness, which is hardness of heart, binds us so tightly to people that we never seem to get out of the wrangle, the arguments and the problems.

Therefore, forgive and forget, and move on. Bless life and be free. The greatest liberation I have achieved in this life is the ability to forgive all people profoundly, deeply and with the totality of my being. It is even possible to forgive those who have committed heinous crimes.

One morning a few years ago, when I had just awakened, I heard my Holy Christ Self forgive the person I thought was my greatest enemy. My Christ Self was setting the example for me. He was showing me, "This is how you must love your enemies."

Of course, this is easier said than done, as we all know. It's not easy to forgive those who have committed crimes against the soul, the mind, the body. So what is the appropriate response to the evildoer?

I prayed to God about this and received an empowering and liberating teaching.

> *In the presence of God, nothing stands between Him and us—we are forgiven. But we cannot feel His presence if anything is allowed to stand between ourselves and others.*
>
> — DAG HAMMARSKJÖLD

Resolution is a two-step process. First, we invoke divine mercy and forgive the soul of the one who committed the wrong, and we also ask God to forgive that soul.

Second, we invoke divine justice for the

binding of the not-self of the wrongdoer. We also ask God to give the soul the opportunity to repent of her deeds and to strengthen herself so she can resist the urge to do wrong when it knocks again at her door. Engaging in this process can help us forgive even those whom we have the hardest time forgiving.

Each night as we lay our bodies down to sleep, it's the end of a cycle and we have a chance to forgive. It's our time to let go of all discord, all problems and to forgive every part of life. We want to turn the page of the day and for it to be finished and resolved.

So we practice forgiveness every day, every night. And as we do, we are taking firm steps toward our goal. For little by little as we work through our emotions (including our anger), forgive ourselves, forgive others and come to resolution, portions of ourselves are daily becoming part of our Higher Self, our Real Self.

Soul Reflections

Extending forgiveness to others

Think of an instance when someone has wronged or hurt you. If it is a painful situation, remember that you can forgive that person's soul.

Ask God to work with that soul. And ask your Higher Self to show you how to forgive that one, including whether you need to take any action.

Try using the following meditation and affirmation.

Imagine a sphere of violet light surrounding those you want to forgive, dissolving all negativity and filling their souls with the light of forgiveness. Then repeat the following affirmation for each one of them, inserting his or her name in the blank:

_____ *is a being of violet fire!*

_____ *is the purity God desires!*

3. Make Friends in Heaven

God fashioned the angels out of his own flaming Presence, creating them before us so we would have caretakers. Angels are ministering servants who tend our spirits, minds, souls and bodies. They help us in countless ways. They protect, guide, strengthen, heal, comfort, teach, counsel and warn us.

I perceive angels as "angles" of God's consciousness. They come in at every point and angle and vector of the universe to deliver their light to us. They especially work with our emotional bodies, intensifying feelings of love, hope, courage, honor, mercy and faith as well as every aspect of the mind of God.

> *Make yourself familiar with the angels, and behold them frequently in spirit; for without being seen, they are present with you.*
>
> – ST. FRANCIS DE SALES

You can make it a goal to become familiar with the angels and archangels. And you can establish such a true and lasting friendship that you feel absolutely comfortable walking and talking with them anytime, anywhere. You can become comfortable giving them assignments and asking for their assistance in the most difficult personal and private matters and in matters of global concern.[5]

Just as we can befriend angels, so we can make friends with the ascended masters, and they can greatly assist us on the spiritual path. Sometimes when we want to master a new skill, we find someone who is accomplished in that field and we become his or her student. We apprentice ourselves to a personal trainer, someone who has taken this road before and can teach us how to avoid the obstacles and reach the goal. We can apply this same approach to our spiritual journey, which has its own rigors and challenges as well as proven techniques for smoother sailing.

Our souls want to learn from those who have already arrived Home. The ascended masters have attained the same spiritual goals that we aspire to, and they can make the trek a lot easier. They can tutor and guide us at inner levels. And they can give us extraordinary assistance in spiritual and practical matters, including individual sponsorship in our field of endeavor.

The masters are spiritual coaches who can help us to overcome our weaknesses and to develop and leverage our strengths. They inspire and guide us to become all that we are meant to be. Each master is a teacher in the truest sense of the word—one who wants us not only to match his or her attainment but to go beyond it. As real teachers and champions of our soul, the masters inspire us to persevere on the homeward path.

So if you haven't already made friends in heaven, you can begin today to invite the angels and ascended masters into your life to help you achieve your spiritual and material goals.

Soul Reflections

1. *Calling to the angels*

The angels are waiting for you to give them assignments. Nothing is too big or too small for them. You can start right now by thinking of some challenge or problem in your home or workplace. The more specific you can be about what you need, the better. Call the angels into action with a quick, simple prayer like:

"Beloved angels, help me to ___(insert details)___ , according to my divine plan."

They will be by your side instantly when you say this with the fervor of your heart. Give your prayer daily until you see results. And know that the angels will give you the best answer they can based on your soul's needs.

NAME OF ARCHANGEL	AREA OF EXPERTISE
Michael	*protection, power, faith, goodwill*
Jophiel	*wisdom, understanding, enlightenment*
Chamuel	*love, compassion, kindness, charity*
Gabriel	*purity, discipline, joy*
Raphael	*truth, science, healing, abundance, vision, music*
Uriel	*service, ministration, peace, brotherhood*
Zadkiel	*mercy, forgiveness, justice, freedom, transmutation*

2. *Apprenticing to a master*

What spiritual master do you feel close to? Gautama Buddha, Krishna or Kuan Yin? Jesus, Padre Pio or Mother Mary? Try to imitate that master's virtues. Pray to that master. In any given situation, ask yourself, What would he do? What choice would she make? You can talk with your master throughout the day. Don't stop knocking on the master's door and asking for teaching about what you need to know to accelerate your self-mastery.

To learn about ascended masters who have volunteered to teach and coach our souls, a good starting point is the book *Lords of the Seven Rays.*[6]

4. Learn While Your Body Sleeps

While your body sleeps at night, your soul has the opportunity to travel in the etheric body to the retreats of the ascended masters in the heaven-world. These magnificent retreats are also called universities of the Spirit. During these visits, your soul can have direct contact with the ascended masters and the angels. They tutor you in their fields of specialization and help you prepare for the next day's challenges.

You don't automatically travel to these retreats when you slip off into sleep, but there are things you can do to help you get there. First, treat your bedroom as a sanctuary of peace, a clutter-free place of positive energy. Second, don't go to bed at night without making your peace with others. Above all, kneel and ask forgiveness for any harm you may have done to anyone that day. Third, give some prayers to the angels asking them to protect you and take your soul to the retreats.

No one knows what makes the soul wake up so happy! Maybe a dawn breeze has blown the veil from the face of God.

– RUMI

Usually, you don't consciously remember these retreat experiences, but they are real. Some people have glimpses of them at inner levels through their soul memory or through their dreams when the door to realms of light opens just a crack.

When you wake up in the morning, you may

The Royal Teton Retreat

The Royal Teton Retreat, congruent with the Grand Teton mountain near Jackson Hole, Wyoming, is a physical-etheric retreat and an ancient focus of great light. It's the principal retreat of the ascended masters on the North American continent. Thousands of souls from every continent journey there in their finer bodies while they sleep to attend large conclaves as well as small classes and tutorials. Many ascended masters frequent this gathering place, while they also maintain specialized courses in their own retreats.

Souls traveling to the etheric retreats can attend classes on topics in many areas of knowledge—spiritual teachings, including the profound truths of all religions; the science of healing, mathematics, music, the laws of alchemy and precipitation; understanding the intricacies of the will of God in politics, religion, business, finance and education. Various courses provide tutoring in subjects like gaining mastery of the emotions and quieting inordinate desire, invoking light for dealing with karma, and anchoring etheric patterns in tangible ways to improve everyday life—patterns of self-reliance in God, the sacred family and God-government.

The Royal Teton Retreat houses council halls where there is continual planning and development of projects to be carried out by souls in embodiment. Many new inventions, scientific formulas, techniques in art and in every field of human endeavor—already developed by the ascended masters—will also be released from this retreat when mankind have demonstrated their predisposition to use them honorably and morally according to the golden rule.

recall the lessons you learned. Or you may awaken with a clear direction. You may feel that the burdens you prayed about the night before are resolved, or you will get up knowing precisely what steps to take to resolve them.

Even if you don't remember your retreat experience, your soul does know and she will act on it. That's why you always need to have one ear listening to the intuitive faculty of your soul—who knows a lot more about you than you do at the conscious level.

Soul Reflections

1. *Going to spiritual retreats at night*

Before you go to bed at night, you can ask the angels to take you to the spiritual retreats. It can be as simple as the following prayer:

Beloved angels of light, in the name of my own Real Self, I ask that you take me in my soul consciousness to the universities of the Spirit to be tutored in ___(fill in the blank)___ . *I thank you and accept it done this hour in full power.*

Some ideas for the blank might be: the next step toward fulfilling my mission; how to resolve a problem with my spouse (or partner, parent, child, co-worker, friend); how to tap into my creativity.

2. *Keeping a journal by your bed*

Keep a journal with pen or pencil handy by your bed. When you wake up in the night or in the morning, immediately record what you remember. It might be what to do for your health, how to ask your boss for a raise, the key to a great invention, or the answer to something you've been wondering about.

Take note of your dreams. Some dreams are encoded material presented symbolically by your Higher Self. Ask your Higher Self to decipher them and show you how to apply their lessons to your current circumstances.[7]

5. Be Aware of the Not-Self

On the road to self-mastery, we need the courage to explore how much of our identity is invested in our true, divine nature and how much

is invested in our lower nature—our not-self. Kab-
balists called this darker side of our nature "the
evil urge." Saint Paul referred to it as "the carnal
mind." In esoteric tradition it is known as the
dweller-on-the-threshold.

The dweller-on-the-threshold sits at the
threshold of self-awareness where the elements of
the subconscious cross the line to the conscious
mind, and the unknown not-self becomes the
known. Once surfaced, the dweller has entered
the realm of the conscious
will. Through the decision-
making faculties of mind and
heart, the soul may choose
to become, or choose to overcome, the components of this
antithesis of her Real Self.

The not-self is like Scot-
land's legendary Loch Ness
monster—now you see it,
now you don't. The monster surfaces every once
in a while and everyone says, "I've seen Nessie, the
monster."

Loch Ness is a deep body of water that could
be said to represent our emotional body, as any

> *It is as hard to
> see one's self as
> to look backwards
> without turning
> around.*
>
> – HENRY DAVID
> THOREAU

body of water does. The surface of the water symbolizes the line between our conscious awareness and everything that is below the surface of awareness. We may sense rumblings and soundings that the not-self is there. Yet until it finally emerges and shows itself, we don't necessarily know what it is. Somehow the marks of identification are missing.

But periodically, our personal Nessie pokes its little head up and then we get a sense of its identity, a glimpse of what's going on beneath the surface. Every once in a while, we catch ourselves in a vibration or mood that we can hardly believe is native to us. We may suddenly become angry, we may notice we have become terribly jealous, we may feel that we have an intense dislike or hatred for someone. It may come out in a moment of social interaction. And then all of a sudden it's gone and things are back to normal.

You have to go after the not-self because it stands between you and your I AM Presence. It is continually positioning itself to outsmart your soul as she learns her lessons and journeys back to God. Sometimes the not-self is right there, ready to come through the door of consciousness.

Every time you get a glimpse of that not-self peering up, you have to recognize it, seize it and look at it for what it is. You do not deny it and you do not suppress it. Once you have identified it, you make a conscious effort to turn around that condition of consciousness. You can do this by working on your psychology, changing your habit patterns and behavior, and praying fervently. At the same time, your Christ Self, the holy angels and the ascended masters can stand guard to prevent the not-self from acting in your world.

Soul Reflections

1. Catching the not-self

Keep a daily lookout—what have you seen of Nessie in your own world? When you catch yourself off guard, you can sometimes see tendencies you don't want as part of yourself—criticism, argumentation, pride, greed. Remember to look within. Look at your actions or lack of action and the reason behind them. Be courageous enough to overcome the dragon in your soul's personal story.

2. *Doing the spiritual work*

You can pray fervently for spiritual assistance to overcome the not-self. When you see Nessie, send an urgent call to the angels and your Higher Self for help:

"Beloved angels and Higher Self, help me! help me! help me! Stand guard and show me when my not-self is acting."

6. Work on Your Psychology

If we want to fulfill our divine plan and make our ascension, working on our psychology is the order of the day. In fact, we reach a point where we can't go any further spiritually unless we deal with our psychology. The same patterns keep coming back and we need to master them in order to move on. Delving into our psychology helps us understand the blocks to our progress. And the spiritual path gives us the strength and connection to God to overcome and transcend our psychological self.

Aside from the psychology we have developed in this and past lives, we also have to deal with the allotment of karma that has been assigned to us. Our psychology and our karma are intertwined. Karma puts us in circumstances that cause us to develop a certain psychology. In turn, our psychology becomes a part of the karma that we have to work through.

It's important to reach the point of adult responsibility where we can say, "I have no one, absolutely no one, to blame for my karma and my psychology except myself. Those whom I have known are responsible for their actions. But I am responsible for how I react to them. I am responsible for what I will do today."

> *People will do anything, no matter how absurd, in order to avoid facing their own soul.*
>
> – CARL JUNG

However, a part of us does not want to get involved in dealing with our psychology, including the notself. Why? Because it is often difficult work, though it can also be extremely rewarding. We may go through records of the past and a great deal of pain before we arrive at resolution and wholeness.

As we engage in this process, we can gain strides by working with a trained therapist who understands the spiritual path. For when we want to create new patterns, it often takes skilled coaching along with profound inner work. I have observed that the soul respects a professional who is qualified to provide this guidance.

Seeking resolution is part of the spiritual work that leads to our soul's union with God. We work on our psychology because we need resolution not only with others but also with our own soul, and our soul needs resolution with our Holy Christ Self.

We may be dysfunctional in a slice of our life and well balanced in other slices of our life. We have strengths in our souls as well as weaknesses. But all of the soul must become whole; because until she is whole, she cannot permanently unite with her Higher Self.

Soul Reflections

1. *Finding the dysfunctional slice*

Take some time to review your present life and sense where your soul might be asking for help.

Do you have a troublesome relationship? Or do you find yourself repeatedly in unwanted circumstances with your job, your finances or some other area of your life? Write some notes in your journal to ponder.

2. *Making a plan*

Offer your soul the help she needs by reading a good self-help book on psychology, working with a professional or taking some other positive step forward. Remember the angels and the ascended masters, your spiritual coaches. If you can't decide what to do, ask them!

3. *Doing the spiritual work*

Often psychological as well as spiritual work are necessary for deep soul healing. Your soul work can be accelerated by applying the spiritual tools in "Daily Meditations and Affirmations to Nurture Your Soul," beginning on page 93. You can try the affirmation below right now. Remember, when you say "I AM," you are affirming God within you, your I AM Presence. Envision light pouring into your unconscious and conscious mind as you say the words:

I AM changing all my garments,
Old ones for the bright new day;
With the sun of understanding
I AM shining all the way.

I AM light within, without;
I AM light is all about.
Fill me, free me, glorify me!
Seal me, heal me, purify me!

 # 7. Talk with God

Y ou can have a direct line to God through prayer—both devotional and invocative prayer. Devotional prayer is giving yourself to God—your whole heart, your soul, your mind. Invocative prayer is invoking the whole heart and soul and mind of God to enter your being.

Prayer is not just a prescribed set of devotions and petitions to God. It is a profound communion wherein we speak with God from the depths of our soul.

In reality, prayer is a conversation. We don't

just reach out to God; God also reaches out to us—
with guidance, comfort, direction and help. Making
a spiritual connection through prayer is what Teresa of Avila called "an intimate sharing between friends." She also warned that just as "family ties and friendship are lost through lack of communication," our relationship with God can be lost if we don't pray.[8]

Prayer feeds the soul—as blood is to the body, prayer is to the soul—and it brings you closer to God.

— MOTHER TERESA

Intense love and feeling for God forges a direct route to him. So if you were to ask me, "What do I have to do to make my ascension?" I would tell you that an essential step is to enter the devotional path with intensity.

Don't just keep the path in your head, but get into the depths of your feeling for God. Get in the habit of walking and talking with him. If you think he's not answering, just keep right on talking to him. He will answer you in good time at the level that you can hear him. In fact, he is always answering you, though you may not hear him.

You may have experienced, for example, the intercession of angels in your life without calling to them or saying a prayer. For your soul has had an ongoing relationship with God and the angels from this and past lives, even though outwardly you may not be aware of it.

Perhaps from the level of the subconscious mind, your soul is crying out to God imploring his assistance, irrespective of what your outer mind is doing. You may not be conscious that your soul is, and has been for a long time, engaged in interior prayer. And God always answers the prayer of the heart, often by sending his ministering angels.

> *Prayer, crystallized in words, assigns a permanent wave length on which the dialogue has to be continued, even when our mind is occupied with other matters.*
>
> — DAG HAMMARSKJÖLD

With daily prayer, you can nourish your soul's connection to your Higher Self and to God. Your conversation with God doesn't have to take long. When I take time first thing in the morning to connect with God through heartfelt prayer, I find that my day is transformed and it goes more smoothly. I don't get caught up in needless distractions and emergencies that pull me away from my goals.

Aside from increasing your soul's attunement and helping you in practical ways, heartfelt prayer is one of the most effective ways to balance karma. So make prayer an integral part of your spiritual path, and experience the joy and acceleration it will bring to your soul.

Soul Reflections

1. *Making a spiritual connection every day*

If you aren't already in the habit, take some time each day, even just fifteen minutes, to pray, meditate or say affirmations out loud. Keep a journal of what you are asking for along with the inspirations and results you receive. The answers may come quickly or they may take a while. Constancy is the key.

2. *Staying connected during the day*

If something gets you down during the day, stop what you're doing and find a private place to regain your spiritual connection. You might do this by closing your eyes for a few moments or by taking a few deep breaths.

Applying these keys can bring profound benefits to your daily life, your relationships and your spiritual path. When you are climbing the mountain to the summit of being, you'll find that "the trek upward is worth the inconvenience."[9]

PART 5

Daily Meditations and Affirmations to Nurture Your Soul

Spending Quality Time with Your Soul

The essential ingredient of the path is to live a spiritual life, cultivating it within (through meditation, heartfelt prayer, devotion) and in your relationship to the world around you (which often includes helping others).

We have access to vast spiritual reserves that can guide us daily, even in practical ways. But we have to make the time to tap into this wellspring of wisdom.

It's difficult to develop Christ consciousness if your mind is involved in human affairs 100 percent of the time. You need time for studying and assimilating spiritual truths. You need time for meditation and reflection, for your soul to commune with God.

Physical renewal also supports your spiritual path. This may mean getting regular exercise, healing the body, fasting, doing whatever you need to maintain your health. Exercise increases the flow of *prana*—the energy that vitalizes all living things. Prana influences the mind, body, spirit and emotions.

> *Be good, keep your feet dry, your eyes open, your heart at peace and your soul in the joy of Christ.*
>
> – THOMAS MERTON

You can use short exercise breaks to commune with God, perhaps giving mantras and affirmations while you're walking. You can use that time to attune with your Holy Christ Self, to ask him questions, to enter into his heart and to send blessings to those in need. Longer periods of spiritual and physical recharge are also helpful in sustaining your spiritual life.

When I go for walks in the beautiful mountains of Montana where I live, I breathe deeply and attune with God and nature. I give my prayers. Whenever I'm in California, I like to walk or jog along the beach and give my mantras.

You, too, can find simple ways to spend time with your soul in the midst of the busyness of life. Be creative!

The Power of Spoken Prayer

Apowerful way to reinforce your personal and heartfelt prayers to God is through the science of the spoken Word. Spoken prayer is at the heart of the world's religions. The science of the spoken Word as the ascended masters teach it is a step-up of the prayer forms of East and West. It combines prayers, mantras, affirmations and meditations with dynamic decrees—powerful spoken petitions to God. And these bring forth a dynamism of energy that we pass through our chakras, our spiritual energy centers, to the entire world.

Prayer, meditation and decrees are all methods of plugging into God and your own Higher Self. There is a time and a place to practice each of these types of devotion. But no matter what path you follow, you can benefit from adding decrees to your spiritual practices. Decrees are the most powerful method of accessing God's light.

The following prayers and affirmations are meant to be given aloud as dynamic decrees. When we meditate, we commune with God. When we pray, we communicate with God and request his help. When we decree, we are communing, communicating and directing God's light into our world to change the circumstances we see around us. We are, in effect, commanding the flow of energy from Spirit to matter.

Many of these decrees and affirmations use the name of God "I AM" to access spiritual power. "I AM" is short for "I AM THAT I AM," the name of God revealed to Moses when he saw the burning bush. "I AM THAT I AM" means "as above, so below—as God is in heaven, so God is on earth within me, within my Higher Self, within my I AM Presence. Right where I stand, the power of God is." So every time you say, "I AM...," you are affirming "God in me is...."

Whatever statement you make that begins with "I AM" will become a reality in your life. If you say, "I am sick. I am tired. I am angry. I am frightened," these things will come to pass. You can change these to positive statements, but directing God's energy through decrees is much more powerful. For decrees go beyond just positive thinking.

As you experiment with the following decrees, keep in mind these principles. First, ancient spiritual traditions as well as modern scientific studies have shown that sound is effective in creating change, even healing. So when we want to draw down the light and energy of God for transformation, giving decrees aloud is indispensable.

Second, we can enhance the power of our prayers when we specifically name and visualize what we want to take place. Whatever we put our attention on, we are charging with energy. The image we hold in our mind's eye is like a blueprint, and our attention is the magnet that attracts the creative energies of Spirit to fill it in.

Third, repetition increases the benefits of spoken prayer. Decrees, fiats and mantras are all meant to be repeated. In the East, people give their mantras over and over, even thousands of times a day. But in the West, we are not accustomed to doing this.

People often ask, "Why should I have to ask God for something more than once?" The answer is that repeating a prayer is not simply making a request again and again. In truth, you are strengthening the power of the request by qualifying it with more of God's light-energy. You can also begin to enter into a state of oneness with God.

The first time you give a decree, you will want to say it slowly and deliberately, endowing each word with intense love for God. There is great power in giving a decree slowly.

A different power comes from gradually increasing the speed and raising the pitch of the decree. As you increase the speed of your decrees, you will find that they are more effective in raising your vibration. The increase in speed should not be artificial. It should feel natural to you; the decree should almost speed itself up.

The goal of all effective decreeing is to unlock the power of your Real Self and to draw God's energy into the physical world.

 ## Invoking Protection for Your Soul

Your soul is fragile. You can look at a newborn baby and see the fragility of your own soul. She needs nourishment and care to desire to live in this world, which can be difficult, hard, even miserable.

Gautama Buddha once said, "You can look the whole world over and never find anyone more deserving of love than yourself." If we want to make lasting changes in our lives, we have to love, nurture and protect our soul—thus enfolding her in these qualities of the light of God.

You can use the following affirmations to wrap your soul in swaddling garments of light.

Tube of Light

The tube of light is a shield of protective white light, about nine feet in diameter, which streams down from the I AM THAT I AM above you and extends beneath your feet (pictured on page 10).

It can guard against energies of malice that may be directed at you—through anger, condemnation, hatred, jealousy. When you are unprotected, these vibrations can make you irritable or depressed. They can even cause you to have accidents.

The white light can also protect us from the pull of the mass consciousness. When we feel exhausted after a trip into the city or after we go shopping, it's often because our energy has been drained. The tube of light helps us to stay centered and at peace.

It's a good idea to give this decree each morning before the hustle and bustle of the day begins.

Visualization and Meditation:

See the dazzling white light from your I AM Presence, brighter than the sun shining on new-fallen snow, coalescing to form an impenetrable wall of light around you. Inside this scintillating tube of light, see yourself enfolded in the violet flame. Throughout the day, you can reinforce this spiritual protection by visualizing the tube of light around you and repeating the decree.

Tube of Light

Beloved I AM Presence bright,
Round me seal your tube of light
From ascended master flame
Called forth now in God's own name.
Let it keep my temple free
From all discord sent to me.

I AM calling forth violet fire
To blaze and transmute all desire,
Keeping on in freedom's name
Till I AM one with the violet flame.

Decrees and Affirmations for Protection

Archangel Michael, the Prince of the Archangels, is the greatest and most revered of angels in Jewish, Christian and Islamic scriptures and traditions. He is a real friend to us. With his legions of light, he has dedicated himself for thousands of years to our protection and to strengthening our will and faith.

Visualization:

As you give the following decree, visualize Archangel Michael and his mighty blue angels all around you. As you say, "I AM his love protecting here," see Archangel Michael protecting everyone on earth.

This is a great decree to give while driving. You can visualize Archangel Michael and his angels surrounding every car on the road. You can also give this decree and visualization anytime you feel the need to protect yourself from harm or negativity.

Traveling Protection

Lord Michael before, Lord Michael behind,
Lord Michael to the right, Lord Michael
    to the left,
Lord Michael above, Lord Michael below,
Lord Michael, Lord Michael wherever I go!
I AM his love protecting here!
I AM his love protecting here!
I AM his love protecting here!

A fiat is a short, powerful exclamatory statement that calls forth God's light. Giving a fiat with fervor and love invokes the assistance of the heavenly hosts. You can use the following fiat to call for the instantaneous protection of Archangel Michael.

Archangel Michael,
Help me! Help me! Help me!

Tell us how you liked this book!

Book title: _____

What did you like the most? _____

_____

Other comments? _____

_____

Other topics of interest? _____

☐ **YES! Send me FREE BOOK CATALOG.** ☐ I'm a seeker—send me more info.

Name _____

Address _____

City _____ State _____ Zip Code _____

E-mail: _____ Phone no. _____

Your tax-deductible contributions make these publications available to the world.

Please make your checks payable to: Summit University Press, 63 Summit Way, Gardiner, MT 59030-9314.
Call us toll free at 1-800-245-5445. Outside the U.S.A., call 406-848-9500.
E-mail: tslinfo@tsl.org   www.SummitUniversityPress.com

491-#7276 SOYS 5/07

ARCHANGEL MICHAEL

The Spiritual Alchemy of the Violet Flame

The violet flame (pictured surrounding the lower figure in the Chart of Your Divine Self on page 10) can elevate and invigorate us. It can contribute to healing emotional and even physical problems, improve relationships and make life more joyful. Most importantly, the violet flame transforms negative energy into positive energy.

The violet flame is a flame of forgiveness and its action is a spiritual alchemy. We have all sinned and sullied our spiritual garments, but the violet flame can cleanse us of that sin.

It is the spiritual light that stimulates mercy, forgiveness and transmutation. To "transmute" is to change something into a higher form. This term was used centuries ago by alchemists who attempted transmutation on a physical level (to transmute base metals into gold) and on a spiritual level (to achieve transformation and eternal life).

The violet flame can indeed create transformation on a physical and spiritual level. It is a high-frequency spiritual energy that separates out the gross elements of our karma from the gold of our True Self and transmutes them so that we can achieve our highest potential.

The violet flame has been called the highest gift of God to the universe. But to receive this gift, it has to be invoked and it has to be experienced. Try experimenting with it. This is your laboratory, you're the alchemist, and you're saying, "I'm trying out this violet flame. And I'm going to see what it will do for me."

I can tell you what it's done for me over the many years I've used it. It has given me my complete liberation—my liberation as a soul, as a being, as a woman; my liberation from my karma and from many lesser states of consciousness, which I have had just like anyone else. I can tell you that when you give a violet-flame mantra, you can feel joy—a tremendous and profound joy. You can feel freedom, light, hope and happiness.

It will take a different amount of time, from a day to several months, for each person to see the results. But if you remain constant, you will begin to feel the effects. Experiment with it. Try giving violet-flame decrees for at least a month, fifteen minutes a day, and note the positive changes that start to take place in your life.

Since a package of karma arrives on our door-step each morning, many people like to give their violet-flame decrees before their day begins. But we can give our decrees anywhere, anytime—in the shower, in our sacred space, while doing chores or before going to bed.

In fact, simply repeating a violet-flame mantra anytime you feel tense, tired or irritated can make a difference. You will get the greatest benefit from the violet flame, however, if you set aside a specific time each day to decree without interruption. A good place to start is to give one or all of the following affirmations and to repeat them as many times as you like.

Visualization:

Visualize the violet flame penetrating in, through and around the people, events and issues you are praying for. See dancing violet flame con-suming negative karma and habit patterns. See violet-colored flame within your heart and in the hearts of those you are concerned about, softening and then melting away any hardness of heart—

transforming anger into compassion, bitterness into sweetness, anxiety into peace—and bathing all in forgiveness.

Violet Flame Mantra

I AM a being of violet fire!
I AM the purity God desires!

A Prayer for Forgiveness

I AM forgiveness acting here,
Casting out all doubt and fear,
Setting men forever free
With wings of cosmic victory.

I AM calling in full power
For forgiveness every hour;
To all life in every place
I flood forth forgiving grace.

I AM the Violet Flame

I AM the violet flame
  In action in me now
I AM the violet flame
  To light alone I bow
I AM the violet flame
  In mighty cosmic power
I AM the light of God
  Shining every hour
I AM the violet flame
  Blazing like a sun
I AM God's sacred power
  Freeing every one

 Decrees to Take Your Soul All the Way Home

The "Heart, Head and Hand Decrees" are an easy, powerful way to set the course of your day. Each set of verses marks a step toward the goal of becoming one with God. And giving all the sections sequentially reminds you that, first and foremost, your soul is on a spiritual journey back to her source.

These decrees help you to celebrate your path of reunion with God and to experience more of his consciousness day by day. You can give each section once, three times or as many times as you like.

Heart

Violet fire, thou love divine,
Blaze within this heart of mine!
Thou art mercy forever true,
Keep me always in tune with you.

Head

I AM light, thou Christ in me,
Set my mind forever free;
Violet fire, forever shine
Deep within this mind of mine.

God who gives my daily bread,
With violet fire fill my head
Till thy radiance heavenlike
Makes my mind a mind of light.

Hand

I AM the hand of God in action,
Gaining victory every day;
My pure soul's great satisfaction
Is to walk the Middle Way.

Tube of Light

Beloved I AM Presence bright,
Round me seal your tube of light
From ascended master flame
Called forth now in God's own name.
Let it keep my temple free
From all discord sent to me.

I AM calling forth violet fire
To blaze and transmute all desire,
Keeping on in freedom's name
Till I AM one with the violet flame.

Forgiveness

I AM forgiveness acting here,
Casting out all doubt and fear,
Setting men forever free
With wings of cosmic victory.

I AM calling in full power
For forgiveness every hour;
To all life in every place
I flood forth forgiving grace.

Supply

I AM free from fear and doubt,
Casting want and misery out,
Knowing now all good supply
Ever comes from realms on high.

I AM the hand of God's own fortune
Flooding forth the treasures of light,
Now receiving full abundance
To supply each need of life.

Perfection

I AM life of God direction,
Blaze thy light of truth in me.
Focus here all God's perfection,
From all discord set me free.

Make and keep me anchored ever
In the justice of thy plan—
I AM the presence of perfection
Living the life of God in man!

Transfiguration

I AM changing all my garments,
Old ones for the bright new day;
With the sun of understanding
I AM shining all the way.

I AM light within, without;
I AM light is all about.
Fill me, free me, glorify me!
Seal me, heal me, purify me!
Until transfigured they describe me:
I AM shining like the Son,
I AM shining like the Sun!

Resurrection

I AM the flame of resurrection
Blazing God's pure light through me.
Now I AM raising every atom,
From every shadow I AM free.

I AM the light of God's full Presence,
I AM living ever free.
Now the flame of life eternal
Rises up to victory.

Ascension

I AM ascension light,
Victory flowing free,
All of good won at last
For all eternity.

I AM light, all weights are gone.
Into the air I raise;
To all I pour with full God power
My wondrous song of praise.
All hail! I AM the living Christ,
The ever-loving One.
Ascended now with full God power,
I AM a blazing Sun!

A Meditation on Being Light

The following decree affirming "I AM Light" is a meditation on your True Self. You can use it to conclude your spiritual exercises, as a preparation for going to sleep at night, or anytime your soul is in need of remembering her divine identity in the midst of daily life.

A thirteenth-century Jewish Kabbalist mystic advised:

> *Whatever one implants firmly in the mind becomes the essential thing. So if you pray and offer a blessing to God, or if you wish your intention to be true, imagine you are light. All around you—in every corner and on every side—is light. Turn to your right, and you will find shining light; to your left, splendor, a radiant light. Between them, up above, the light of the Presence. Surrounding that, the light of life. Above it all, a crown of light—crowning the aspirations of thought,*

*illumining the paths of imagination,
spreading the radiance of vision. This
light is unfathomable and endless.*[10]

Visualization and Meditation:

Imagine you are light. See the cosmic white-
fire radiance infilling and surrounding you. As
thoughts arise, just release them into this light.
And see what the light can do for you—how it can
strengthen your body, mind and spirit.

As you give this decree, meditate upon your
soul's union with her Higher Self and I AM Presence and her return Home from her long journey.

I AM Light

*I AM light, glowing light,
Radiating light, intensified light.
God consumes my darkness,
Transmuting it into light.*

*This day I AM a focus of the Central Sun.
Flowing through me is a crystal river,
A living fountain of light
That can never be qualified
By human thought and feeling.*

I AM an outpost of the Divine.
Such darkness as has used me is swallowed up
By the mighty river of light which I AM!

I AM, I AM, I AM light;
I live, I live, I live in light.
I AM light's fullest dimension;
I AM light's purest intention.
I AM light, light, light
Flooding the world everywhere I move,
Blessing, strengthening, and conveying
The purpose of the kingdom of heaven.

There are pearls in the deep sea, but one must hazard all to find them. If diving once does not bring you pearls, you need not therefore conclude that the sea is without them. Dive again and again. You are sure to be rewarded in the end. So is it with the finding of the Lord in this world. If your first attempt proves fruitless, do not lose heart. Persevere in your efforts. You are sure to realize him at last.

—SRI RAMAKRISHNA

Notes

1. This story is based on "The Hymn of the Pearl." See Bentley Layton, *The Gnostic Scriptures* (Garden City, N.Y.: Doubleday and Co., 1987), pp. 371–75. See also Elizabeth Clare Prophet, *Reincarnation: The Missing Link in Christianity,* pp. 138–40.* In the original text of "The Hymn of the Pearl," the distant land representing the material world in which we live, the plane of mortality, was called "Egypt."

2. See Exod. 3:13–15.

3. See Rev. 22:1.

4. Zohar 1:99b, in Harry Sperling, Maurice Simon, and Paul P. Levertoff, trans., *The Zohar,* 5 vols. (London: Soncino Press, 1934), 1:324. Quoted in Elizabeth Clare Prophet, *Kabbalah: Key to Your Inner Power,* p. 119.

5. See *How to Work with Angels,* by Elizabeth Clare Prophet.

6. See *Lords of the Seven Rays: Mirror of Consciousness,* by Mark L. Prophet and Elizabeth Clare Prophet.

7. To assist in decoding your dreams, see Marilyn C. Barrick, *Dreams: Exploring the Secrets of Your Soul.*

*Unless otherwise noted, all books are published by Summit University Press.

8. *The Book of Her Life* 8.5 and *The Way of Perfection* 26:9, in *Collected Works of St. Teresa of Avila,* trans. Kieran Kavanaugh and Otilio Rodriquez (Washington, D.C.: ICS Publications, 1976), 1:67, 2:136.

9. "The trek upward is worth the inconvenience." El Morya, Keepers of the Flame Lesson 3.

10. Daniel C. Matt, *God and the Big Bang: Discovering Harmony between Science and Spirituality* (Woodstock, Vt.: Jewish Lights Publishing, 1996), p. 73. Quoted in Elizabeth Clare Prophet, *Kabbalah,* p. 249.

SUMMIT UNIVERSITY 🔥 PRESS®

Karma and Reincarnation

Transcending Your Past, Transforming Your Future

The word *karma* has made it into the mainstream. But not everyone understands what it really means or how to deal with it. This insightful book will help you come to grips with karmic connections from past lives that have helped create the circumstances of your life today. You'll discover how your actions in past lives—good and bad—affect which family you're born into, who you're attracted to, and why some people put you on edge. You'll learn about group karma, what we do between lives, and how to turn your karmic encounters into grand opportunities to shape the future you want.

ISBN: 978-0-922729-61-6
224 pages $6.95

Soul Mates and Twin Flames

The Spiritual Dimension of Love and Relationships

"After thirty-five years as a relationship counselor, I find *Soul Mates and Twin Flames* to be extremely powerful in revealing the inner mysteries of the soul and the true essence of love through its insightful analysis of real-life experiences and classical love stories."

—MARILYN C. BARRICK, Ph.D.,
author of *Sacred Psychology of Love*

ISBN: 978-0-922729-48-7
166 pages $6.95

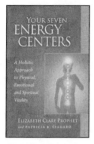

ISBN: 978-0-922729-56-2
234 pages $6.95

Your Seven Energy Centers
A Holistic Approach to Physical, Emotional and Spiritual Vitality

"What is so beautiful about this book is that it can speak to everyone about revitalization and inner peace."

—MAGICAL BLEND MAGAZINE

"Marries ancient healing wisdom with practical spiritual insights to help you create your own dynamic and uniquely personal healing journey. Your 21st-century guide to integrating and healing body, mind and soul."

—ANN LOUISE GITTLEMAN, author of *The Living Beauty Detox Program*

"A small book with a big message.... This handy little guide is packed with useful insights."

—WHOLE LIFE TIMES

ISBN: 978-0-922729-60-9
204 pages $6.95

Alchemy of the Heart
How to Give and Receive More Love

"There is no way you can read this book and not feel more love for those around you—and as you do, you can see the healing changes that love will bring."

—MAGICAL BLEND MAGAZINE

"Through this 'pocket guide to practical spirituality' we learn the alchemical means to heal and empower our hearts, fulfill our reason for being, and extend our capacity to love. In other words, we learn how we can become 'a living transformer of love.'"

—BODHI TREE BOOK REVIEW

How to Work with Angels

"Angels—and our relationship to them—are neither a trend nor a fad.... Ultimately, one's relationship with an angel is a personal one, and in *How to Work with Angels*, you'll discover how to make angels more present in your life.... Whether for love, healing, protection, guidance, or illumination, angels stand ready to help you in many practical and personal ways.... Also included here are a collection of visualizations, affirmations, prayers and decrees." —BODHI TREE BOOK REVIEW

ISBN: 978-0-922729-41-8
118 pages $6.95

Creative Abundance

Keys to Spiritual and Material Prosperity

"*Creative Abundance* contains keys for magnetizing the spiritual and material abundance we all need. Its sensible step-by-step techniques—including treasure mapping, principles of feng shui, meditations, visualizations and affirmations—show how to live a full and prosperous life."

—BODHI TREE BOOK REVIEW

ISBN: 978-0-922729-38-8
174 pages $6.95

FOR MORE INFORMATION

Summit University Press books are
available at fine bookstores worldwide and at
your favorite online bookseller. Our books
are translated into more than 25 languages.
If you would like to receive a free catalog
featuring our books and products,
please contact:

SUMMIT UNIVERSITY PRESS
63 Summit Way
Gardiner, MT 59030-9314 USA

1-800-245-5445 or 406-848-9500

E-mail: info@summituniversitypress.com

www.PocketGuidesToPracticalSpirituality.com

www.bookstudygroups.org

Children's spiritual lessons:

www.pathwayforfamilies.org

ELIZABETH CLARE PROPHET
is a world-renowned author.
Among her bestselling titles
are *Fallen Angels and the
Origins of Evil, The Lost
Years of Jesus,* The Lost
Teachings of Jesus series,
*Kabbalah: Key to Your
Inner Power, Reincarnation:*

The Missing Link in Christianity, and her Pocket
Guides to Practical Spirituality series, which in-
cludes *Your Seven Energy Centers, Karma and
Reincarnation, Alchemy of the Heart,* and *Soul
Mates and Twin Flames.*

She has pioneered techniques in practical
spirituality, including the creative power of sound
for personal growth and world transformation.

A wide selection of her books have been translated into more than 25 languages and are sold
worldwide.

Mrs. Prophet retired in 1999 and is now living
in Montana's Rocky Mountains. The unpublished
works of Mark L. Prophet and Elizabeth Clare
Prophet continue to be published by Summit
University Press.